A Discovery Biography

Sam Houston

CHELSEA JUNIORS
A division of Chelsea House Publishers
New York ◆ Philadelphia

The Discovery Biographies have been prepared under the
educational supervision of Mary C. Austin, Ed.D.,
Reading Specialist and Professor of Education, Case
Western Reserve University.

Cover illustration: Jerry Teters

First Chelsea House edition 1991

1 3 5 7 9 8 6 4 2

ISBN 0-7910-1441-X

Contents

Sam Houston: Hero of Texas

CHAPTER

1	"Call Me 'Captain'!" . . .	7
2	The Raven	15
3	I O U	23
4	"Well, Sam?"	27
5	"He Won't Last the Night" .	33
6	"You're Starting Late!" . .	39
7	"A Man I Can Trust" . . .	45
8	Santa Anna	51
9	The Alamo	57
10	San Jacinto	65
11	Two Monuments	75

Chapter *1*

"Call Me 'Captain'!"

Sam waved his wooden sword and shouted "Halt!"

He had six boys in his army. His little brother Willie was youngest. He was five. His friend Tom was oldest. He was nine, one year older than Sam.

But Sam was captain. He was bigger than Tom. Besides, he knew how to run an army. He was the son of a soldier.

Father had fought in the Revolutionary War. He had helped America beat the British.

Lots of fathers and grandfathers had fought in the war. But they were not soldiers now. It was 1801, eighteen years since the war ended in 1783. Most men left the army then. But Father was still a soldier. He was Captain Sam Houston. He wasn't home very much. He rode from one fort to another. He had to see if the soldiers were doing things right.

Father had taught Sam to read out of *The Manual of Arms*. That was a book that told how to train soldiers. Sam could read "Halt!" and "Forward march!" and "Charge!" before he started to school.

Father called him, "The best soldier of your size in Virginia!"

Sam always saluted and said, "I'll be the next Captain Sam Houston!"

Every day Sam drilled his army around Timber Ridge. That was what Father called his big plantation. Sam marched his army from the little stone church to the log schoolhouse. He marched them from the big white house to the woods. He always drilled them until time for school.

"Mark time!" he yelled. "One, two!" The boys stamped their feet.

Tom stopped. "Hey, Sam!"

"Call me 'Captain'!"

"Yes, sir. Hey, Captain! We're going to be late for school!"

Sam looked up at the sun. "Forward!

Forward, my brave men! To the school-house! Charge!"

The boys ran. Sam could have beaten them. He waited for Willie.

Willie grabbed Sam's hand. "Captain, sir, are we going to be late *again?*"

"Don't worry. I'll take the blame."

"What will the teacher say *this* time?"

Sam could guess what the teacher would say. "Sam Houston! Why can't you be like your older brothers? Why don't you set an example for Willie?"

It was hard to be the middle child of nine. Paxton and Robert and James and John were older. Willie and Mary and Isabelle and Eliza Ann were younger. Every day somebody said, "Mind your older brothers! Set an example for Willie!"

The boys had reached the schoolhouse. They waited for Sam. Just as Sam got there, the teacher opened the door. "Well, Sam?"

"It's my fault, sir."

The teacher sighed. "Sam Houston! Why can't you be like your older brothers? I don't know what will become of you!"

"I know," Sam thought. "I'll be the next Captain Houston." But he did not say it. He said again, "It's my fault, sir." He led his army into the school.

Two years later Father became Major Houston. Sam was proud enough to burst. Someday *he* would be the *next* Major Houston. Maybe someday soon he would ride to the forts with Father.

In 1807, when Sam was fourteen, Father died suddenly. After the funeral Mother called the children together. She said to them, "Father owed a lot of money. He sold Timber Ridge to pay his debts. All we have left is some land in Tennessee." She looked at her family. "We will go there and start a new life. I know you'll help all you can. I know you'll mind Robert."

Sam thought, "Robert will be bossing me." Robert was nineteen. Paxton was older, but he was sick. He had a bad cough. Every day he was paler and thinner.

Robert looked at Sam. "Well, Sam? How about it?"

Sam took a deep breath. He saluted. "Yes, sir!"

Chapter *2*

The Raven

Sam said "Yes, sir!" to Robert all the way to Knoxville, Tennessee. He said "Yes, sir!" through the little town of Maryville. He said "Yes, sir!" till they reached Father's land. It was ten miles from Maryville. Sam looked around him at all the trees. It would be fun to live in the woods.

"Now," Robert said, "we *really* get to work."

Sam threw back his shoulders again. "Yes, sir!"

He helped cut down trees to build their home. They built two log cabins with a roofed-over place between them. They plowed. They planted corn. Soon green shoots poked through the ground.

Robert gave Sam a hoe. "You'll take care of the corn, Sam. Keep the weeds chopped out."

Sam yelled, "No! I hate farming! Why do I have to do it?"

"James and John must help me clear more land. You've got to do something to be worth your salt."

"I won't be a farmer!"

Robert thought a minute. He said, "Mr. Weber wants a clerk in his store in Maryville. Can we depend on you to do that?"

"Anything's better than farming."

16

But working in the store was worse. Sam hated to be shut in all day. He hated to sweep and weigh.

Finally Sam ran off. He didn't take anything but some food, his favorite books and his musket.

Four days later he was in a Cherokee Indian village which was on Hiwassee Island in the Hiwassee River. Most of these Cherokees could speak English. They lived in log houses and raised corn, beans and squash. But Sam did not see any men hoeing corn.

Chief Oo-loo-te-ka said, "So you want to live here. What can you do?"

Sam slapped his gun. "I can fight."

Oo-loo-te-ka said, "We live at peace. My name means *He-Puts-the-Drum-Away.*"

"I can hunt."

Oo-loo-te-ka shook his head. "A musket makes too much noise. You would scare the game." He pointed to a slim tree. "Hit it three times."

Sam shot and hit the tree. He started to reload his musket.

"Quickly!" Oo-loo-te-ka said.

"Just as soon as I've loaded it again!"

An Indian boy shot five arrows into the tree. They were in a straight line, one under the other. Sam wasn't ready to fire his second shot yet. The boy handed Sam his bow and an arrow.

Sam pulled back on the bowstring. He stopped in surprise. How stiff the bow was! He jerked back on the string. The arrow slipped from his fingers. It missed the tree by a yard.

The Indian men said nothing. A little boy of nine or ten looked at Sam with dancing eyes.

Sam pointed to the boy's small bow. "Let's see you shoot."

"My arrows cannot go as far." The little boy went closer to the tree. He shot. His arrow hit the tree in line with the others.

Sam grinned at him. "Little brother, *you* shall teach me to shoot!"

Suddenly all of the Indians were smiling.

Oo-loo-te-ka lifted his hand. "Hear me! This is my son, Co-lon-neh." He said, "That means 'The Raven.' It is a good-luck bird of my people."

Sam bowed. "The Raven shall try to be worthy of his name."

"Can The Raven run?" Oo-loo-te-ka asked.

Sam grinned. He pointed to a tree about 100 yards away. Four boys lined up to race. Sam beat them all.

The Indians cheered.

"How far can my son run in a day?" Oo-loo-te-ka asked.

"In a *day*? I never *tried* to run a whole day. How far can your men run?"

"Twenty-five miles. Our best runners can do better. They can run 50 miles in a day."

"Little Brother," Sam said, "you can teach me to run too."

The Indians laughed. Sam knew they were laughing with him and not at him. He laughed too. He felt at home.

Chapter **3**

I O U

That fall the whole village went hunting. By then Sam could use a bow and arrow. He could run all day. He could move through the forest as quietly as an Indian.

One day in November a tall boy walked into the store in Maryville. He wore buckskin trousers and moccasins. He was almost as brown as an Indian.

His hair was long. A headband kept it out of his eyes. His hair was brown and his eyes were gray.

Mr. Weber stared. "Sam Houston!"

"My name is The Raven." Sam laid two deerskins on the counter. He gave Mr. Weber a slip of paper. "The Raven will buy these things with his deerskins."

Mr. Weber read the list. "Your deerskins will not pay for all these things. You'll still owe 35 dollars."

"I must have presents for my friends." Sam wrote on a piece of paper. "I O U $35.00. Sam Houston." He said, "Next time The Raven shall bring more skins."

Mr. Weber rubbed his chin. "I guess it's all right. Your brothers are part owners of the store now. I guess they'll pay your debts if you don't."

"The Raven will pay his own debts!"

From time to time Sam came back to the store. He brought more skins. He bought more presents. He signed more I O U's.

Three years passed. Again Sam came to the store. Two Indian boys were with him. They were tall, but they did not come to Sam's chin. Sam was over six feet tall.

"The Raven has brought his brothers to help carry his presents," Sam said.

Two men in the store whispered.

Mr. Weber said, "No, Sam. No more presents. Not till you pay what you owe. One hundred dollars."

"What!"

Behind Sam a man laughed. "What you going to do, Mr. Indian?"

Sam did not answer. He walked out of the store with his friends. "Tell Oo-loo-te-ka that The Raven must stay here for a while. He must pay a debt. Then he will come back." He watched the boys walk away.

A man across the street called, "Hey, Mr. Indian! Hear you're in a little trouble!"

Sam did not answer. He started home. That night he sat at his mother's table. He tried to eat. The food stuck in his throat.

After supper Robert said, "Well, Sam? What are you going to do?"

Chapter *4*

"Well, Sam?"

For a long time Sam didn't answer. He was afraid to speak. He didn't know what might happen. He might yell at Robert. He might bawl like a baby.

Robert said again, "Well, Sam? What are you going to do?"

Sam said quietly, "I'll pay my debt."

"How?"

"I don't know yet. But I'll pay it."

Willie smiled. "He'll do it, all right. Sam can do anything he sets his mind to!"

"Thank you, Willie."

Willie was fifteen now. He was stringing up like a weed. He was going to the Porter Academy in Maryville. Everybody said he was doing fine.

"Next week," Willie said, "we're going to have a party in Maryville. People will come from all over the county. We'll have speeches and music and a spelling bee. Wouldn't you like to come?"

Sam looked at his buckskin trousers and moccasins.

Mother said, "We'll make you a new suit."

A week later Sam had a new suit of homespun. The shoemaker in Maryville had made shoes for him. How stiff they felt!

He went to the party. As he walked in he heard a buzz of whispers.

"Hey, Mr. Indian," a man asked, "do you know white man's talk?"

Some people laughed.

"I'll bet I read more in a week than he reads in a year," Sam thought. He had read his favorite books over and over. He knew whole pages by heart. He smiled at the man. "If I hear any words I don't know, I'll ask you."

The last thing on the program was the spelling bee. Willie was one of the captains to choose up sides.

"I want my brother Sam."

A man said, "Too bad to waste your first choice. He won't last long."

When the spelling bee ended, Sam had won.

People clapped. Someone said, "You ought to be a teacher!"

Sam spoke before he thought. "That's what I'm going to do—open a school."

The buzz of whispers began again.

A man said, "I might send my kids to you, if you're cheap enough. *Real* teachers charge six dollars a year. What'll you charge?"

Sam had held his temper a long time. He shouted, "I'll charge eight dollars!"

The day came when Sam opened his school. He stood in an empty log cabin and waited. What was going to happen? Would anybody come?

Chapter *5*

"He Won't Last the Night"

Soon the schoolhouse was crowded. More pupils came. Sam had to turn them away. "I can pay my debt!" he thought. "Next year I'll be back at Hiwassee Island! Nothing can stop me!"

But something did stop him. That summer the War of 1812 began. America was fighting Great Britain again. The next spring Sam joined the army.

Mother did not weep when she said good-by. She gave Sam his father's musket. "Never disgrace it, Sam. Never turn your back to save your life."

"I promise!" And Private Sam Houston marched away. He was only a common soldier now. But someday he would make his mother proud of him!

Before long an officer noticed Sam. After all, Sam did know *The Manual of Arms* by heart. Soon he was Sergeant Houston, drilling other men.

The spring of 1814 he was Ensign Houston. He was going into his first battle. He was fighting under General Andrew Jackson. Jackson's men said he was the best leader in the war. They said Jackson was as "tough as hickory." They called him "Old Hickory."

Old Hickory was fighting the Creek Indians. The Creeks were fighting for the British. They had attacked a fort and killed every man, woman and child. Old Hickory had been after them for months.

Now 1000 Creek warriors were holed up at Horseshoe Bend on the Tallapoosa River. On two sides and behind, the deep river protected them. Across the open end of Horseshoe Bend the Creeks had built a thick breastwork of logs. For two hours Old Hickory's cannons hammered at it. They could not break through.

Now the drums beat the signal, "Charge!"

Sam was the first man over the wall. He slashed his sword right and left.

More men followed him. The Indians began to fall back. They hid in gullies and behind trees and rocks. They went on shooting.

Suddenly Sam realized he had been wounded. An arrow was sticking in his left leg above the knee. He tried to pull it out. He could not. He knew the arrow was barbed, like a fishhook. He turned to a soldier.

"Pull it out."

The soldier tried. "I can't."

Sam lifted his sword. *"Pull it out!"*

The soldier shut his eyes and jerked. The arrow came out. Blood spurted. Men helped Sam over the wall. They tied up the wound to stop the bleeding. They carried him away from the fighting and laid him on the ground.

They went back to the fight. Sam tried to follow them, but he was too dizzy.

Late in the afternoon he got up, gritted his teeth, and limped back to the battle. The Indians were making one last stand. They were in a gully, behind another breastwork of logs.

"I'll not ask the men to charge," Old Hickory said. "I'll ask for volunteers."

Sam ran toward the breastwork. Two bullets hit his right side, one in the shoulder and one in his arm.

The next thing he knew it was dark. Someone was working on his arm.

"Got the bullets out, Doc?" someone asked.

"One. No use going after the other. He won't last the night. He's lost too much blood."

Chapter *6*

"You're Starting Late!"

"I won't die," Sam muttered. *"I won't!"*

In the morning he was still alive. He heard men talking. What could they do with him? He'd never last to Fort Williams, they said. But they couldn't leave him here. Some men put him on a stretcher and started off.

Two months later soldiers brought him to his mother's house.

Mother looked at him, puzzled. Then she gasped, "Sam! It's you!"

Weeks passed before he could sit up. More weeks passed before he could walk. "I've got to get well faster!" he said. "I've got to get back to the army! If I don't, they'll dismiss me."

A letter came for Sam. He had been promoted to a lieutenant. There was a note from General Jackson, too. Old Hickory remembered him. For the first time Sam grinned.

Early in 1815 the war ended. The army began to dismiss men left and right. They dismissed Sam's whole regiment. But they did not dismiss Sam. They sent him to another regiment.

"Maybe," Sam thought, "Old Hickory still remembers me."

Later in 1817 a major sent for Sam. "Lieutenant Houston, I have special orders for you. General Jackson says you're the man for the job."

Old Hickory still remembered him!

"The United States has bought land from the Cherokees. But we're having trouble with some of the chiefs. They won't move west and give up the land. Of course, we could send a regiment in and *make* them go. But we don't want that. You're to talk to them. Get them to go peaceably. You'll leave at once for Hiwassee Island."

Sam wanted to shout, "No!" But he could not. He was a soldier. He had his orders. He went.

"My son!" Oo-loo-te-ka said. "You have come home." He paused. "But a cloud hangs over my son. What is it?"

Sam told him.

Sam carried out his orders. The Indians moved west to the Arkansas River country.

In June of 1818 Sam was in Nashville. He stood in the law office of Mr. James Trimble.

"You want to become a lawyer?" Mr. Trimble stared. "I thought you were in the army."

"I resigned, sir."

"Odd. I heard you were doing very well. How old are you?"

"Twenty-five, sir."

"You're starting late." Mr. Trimble looked up at the rows of heavy books.

"Well, you may read law in my office. But it'll be a long time before you'll be ready to pass your examinations."

"How long, sir?"

"At least eighteen months. Maybe you'll be ready by the end of 1819. You'll be almost 27 then, and not even started. Just ready to start."

"Eighteen months . . ."

"*If* you work hard," Mr. Trimble said. "Very hard."

"Don't worry, sir. I'm going to work!"

Chapter 7

"A Man I Can Trust"

Sam passed his law examinations in six months. Before the end of 1819 he was Attorney General of the Nashville District and Colonel Houston of the Tennessee Militia.

In 1823 Major General Houston was in Washington, a congressman from Tennessee. In 1827 he was Governor of his state.

By 1828 people were talking of bigger things for Sam. Old Hickory had been elected President. "You'll be the next President, Sam," men said. "Nothing can stop you!"

But early in 1829 a tall, bearded man rode into Oo-loo-te-ka's village on the Arkansas River.

"My son!" the old chief said.

"The Raven has come home."

Oo-loo-te-ka did not ask questions. But that night Sam told him. "I have not told this to any white man. I never shall. But I tell you. Not long ago I was married. Then I found out my wife loved someone else. Her family had made her marry me, because they thought I might be the next President of the United States."

"The Raven is welcome as long as he wants to stay."

Sam said, "The Raven will never again walk among white men."

But three years later Sam went to Washington. He went for the sake of the Cherokees. He told Old Hickory how some of the government agents had been cheating the Cherokees.

Old Hickory checked on the agents He fired several. Then he asked, "Now what are you going to do, Sam?"

"I'll go back to the Cherokees. They need me."

"I need you too, Sam. I need a man I can trust. I want you to go to Texas for me."

He told Sam what had happened in Texas. Texas was ruled by Mexico.

But the Mexicans had never settled much of the land. They had trouble with the Indians. So they let people from other countries settle in Texas.

"It's been a good bargain for the Mexicans," Old Hickory said. "The settlers have fought the Indians for them. A great many of our people have gone to Texas and become Mexican citizens. It looked like a bargain to them. They got good land for very little money. But things have been going from bad to worse. The rulers of Mexico have been regular tyrants."

"Why do the Texans put up with them?" Sam asked.

"There are less than 30,000 Texans, and there arc about 8,000,000 Mexicans," Old Hickory said. "Texas has no army.

If war began, I know what would happen. Many volunteers would come a-running. They'd fight a battle or two. Then they would go home. You can't win a war that way. I went through that sort of trouble in the War of 1812. Only trained soldiers will stick. Only trained men will obey."

"What do you think I can do in Texas?" Sam asked.

"Be my eyes and ears. Find out how the Texans feel. Find out what's going to happen."

Chapter 8

Santa Anna

The eyes and ears of Old Hickory.
Sam rode slowly toward a town called
Nacogdoches in eastern Texas. "First, I
must get to know the people," he
thought. "That will take time. Then—"

"Sam Houston!" a man called. It
was a man from Tennessee.

In half an hour Sam was talking
with three dozen men. "We need you,"
they said.

Sam felt a warm glow. "Why?"

Then an argument started. Texas seemed to be split into a "Peace Party" and a "War Party."

The men from the Peace Party said, "Sam, you have been a congressman and a governor. You can help us get along with Mexico."

The men from the War Party said, "Bah! You can help us fight against the Mexicans!"

"Do you have an army?" Sam asked.

They laughed. "Don't you worry. Any Texan can lick 50 Mexicans."

Sam promised to come back. He rode west. He stopped in towns along the way. He went as far as San Antonio. When he got back to Nacogdoches he had ridden over 1000 miles.

But how little he'd seen of Texas! A man could ride for a year and never see half of it. He stopped just outside Nacogdoches. He drew a deep breath. Texas was the place for him. He'd never feel shut in. Here a man could start a new life.

He rode into Nacogdoches. "I've come to stay."

He became a Texan. He opened a law office. He wrote to Old Hickory how he felt about Texas. He ended his letter, "I believe nine-tenths of the Texans want to rebel against Mexico. If they won their independence they would want to join the United States."

"*If* they won their independence," he thought. How could they ever do that?

In the fall of 1835, war began.

General Santa Anna was the President of Mexico then. He sent a regiment into Texas with orders: All Texans were to give up their guns. Any man found bearing arms would be shot.

Even the Peace Party shook fists and yelled. Texans depended on hunting for much of their food. How could they hunt without guns? How could they protect themselves against Indian raids?

Texans called a convention. Every town sent a man. Nacogdoches sent Sam. The convention elected him Commander-in-Chief of their army.

"What army?" Sam thought.

Volunteers did not wait for an army to be organized. They "came a-running." They fought the Mexicans and drove them out. Hurrah! The war was over!

"The war has not even begun!" Sam told them. "Santa Anna will come. He will wait till spring when the grass is up. He will need food for his horses and mules. But he'll come by March 1. We must be ready for him!"

The volunteers said "Bah!" Over 200 men went south with Dr. Grant and Colonel Johnson. They were going to capture Matamoros in Mexico. Other volunteers went home.

Sam argued. He pleaded. He swore. The government got tired of him. They made Colonel Fannin the Commander-in-Chief.

They ordered Sam north. He was to talk to the Indians in northeastern Texas. He was to get their promise that they would not help the Mexicans.

Chapter *9*

The Alamo

Sam rode north. His friend Major Hockley rode with him.

At last Hockley spoke. "Can you get back in time for the next convention? It meets March 1 at Washington-on-the-Brazos."

"I bet they are hoping I can't."

They found the Cherokees. Sam got their promise not to help the Mexicans.

He and Hockley started back at a gallop. Hockley's horse went lame.

Sam didn't stop. "I'll see you in Washington-on-the-Brazos!" he yelled.

On March 1 Sam strode into the convention.

Men jumped up, and they crowded around him. Were they going to throw him out?

"General Houston! Thank heaven you're here!" Sam had been right, they said. Santa Anna had come. He was attacking the Alamo. Colonel Travis and 150 Texans were trapped there.

"Oh, no!" Sam had seen the Alamo. It was a mission near San Antonio. Sometimes the Alamo was used as a fort. Travis could never hold it with 150 men. "What have you done?"

"He sent a call for help. We hope our men have answered it."

"What men?" Sam asked. "Where are Grant and Johnson? On their way to Mexico?"

"They gave that up. Too many men deserted. Last we heard, they were hunting wild horses."

"Where's your Commander-in-Chief?"

Men looked at their boots. "Fannin's at Goliad. We're *sure* he's gone to help Travis. And Fannin has 400 men, all trained soldiers, from the United States."

"I know," Sam said. "They're men I sent for."

Again the men studied their boots.

The next day the Texans declared their independence from Mexico. They set to work to organize a government.

They re-elected Sam Commander-in-Chief. Another message came from the Alamo. Only 32 men had answered the call for help. They were from Gonzales, a town 70 miles from the Alamo. Fannin had sent no men. So Travis had fewer than 200 soldiers. He was running out of ammunition.

Sam sent orders to Grant and Johnson and Fannin: "Join me at Gonzales!" He galloped out of town. Hockley and three others rode along.

At dawn the next morning Sam put his ear to the ground. He listened. "We're too late. If they were still fighting I could hear the guns. The Alamo has fallen. *Come on!*"

Near Gonzales the road was crowded with Texans carrying guns.

"We heard there was shooting again," one man said. "So we came a-running. Where's the fight?"

Sam said, "Major Hockley, get these men organized. Start drilling them!" He dashed on alone into the town.

People crowded around him. Was there any news from the Alamo?

"No word yet," Sam told them.

Four days later they knew. Santa Anna had killed every man at the Alamo. Now he would march on Gonzales. He had 7000 men.

A scout brought word of Grant and Johnson. A Mexican army had attacked them. A few of their soldiers had escaped. The rest of the men were dead.

Sam could wait no longer for Fannin. He must leave Gonzales right away.

He sent Fannin orders where to meet him. That night Gonzales was empty. The army moved slowly. They had to take care of the townspeople.

A scout brought more bad news. Fannin would not come. He was going to hold Goliad.

"Hockley," Sam said, "we'll never see poor Fannin again. Get ready to march."

He looked at his rag-taggle army. It was the last hope of Texas. He could not risk a battle yet. He must retreat. How the Texans were going to hate that!

Chapter *10*

San Jacinto

Sam marched his men in a crazy zigzag, north, then east, then south, then north again. He had to dodge the armies he could not beat. "We came to *fight!*" the men said. Some deserted.

One night a ragged soldier crawled into Sam's camp. He had been one of Fannin's men. Fannin had finally started out from Goliad. But it had been too late. A Mexican army had surrounded him.

"We surrendered," the man whispered. "They marched us back to Goliad. Then Santa Anna sent orders to shoot us. They marched us out of the town and shot us down like dogs. I got away. I don't know if any others did."

That night 100 men deserted.

Now and then more volunteers joined. Once Sam had 600 men. What chance would they have against 7000?

One thing gave Sam hope. Santa Anna's armies were not together. They were spread out on a front 100 miles wide.

Still Sam retreated and did not fight. More men deserted. Other volunteers joined him. At last, on April 21, 1836, he faced Santa Anna by the San Jacinto River. Sam had fewer than 800 men.

Santa Anna had more than 1300. He had made a barricade of baggage and wagons in front of his camp.

The Texans knew the time had come to fight. Why didn't General Houston give the order to attack? All day they grumbled and waited. It was after three o'clock when Sam called them together. He gave them their orders. He gave them a battle cry, too: *"Remember the Alamo! Remember Goliad!"*

The Texans started silently across the plain toward Santa Anna's camp. Sam rode back and forth in front of them. "Hold your fire! Hold your fire!"

The Mexicans fired. Sam's horse fell. He yelled again, "Hold your fire!" He mounted another horse. He raced back and forth, yelling, "Hold your fire!"

That horse fell too. "Hold your fire!" Sam mounted a third horse. At last he yelled, "Remember the Alamo! Fire!"

The Texans had caught the Mexicans off guard. They were lounging around camp. Some were playing cards. Some were asleep. The battle did not last half an hour. The Mexicans surrendered.

Sam rode back to his camp. Suddenly he was dizzy. Hockley grabbed him as he fell from his saddle.

The next thing Sam knew a doctor was working on his leg. "Both bones are smashed," the doctor said, "just above the ankle."

"Did we get Santa Anna?" Sam asked.

No, his men said, there was no sign of him.

"Keep hunting! Look for someone dressed as a common soldier. He'll probably be crawling away on all fours."

The next day Sam's men brought in one more Mexican. He looked like a common soldier. But the other prisoners gasped, *"El Presidente!"*

A roar went up from the Texans. They knew *"El Presidente"* meant "The President." They had captured Santa Anna! Hurrah! Texas was free! The war was over!

The doctor was frowning at Sam's leg. "We've got to get you to New Orleans. We can't take care of you here."

"I can't leave," Sam said. "I have things to do."

It was a month later when Sam got to New Orleans. The doctor there swore when he saw the leg.

Three weeks later the doctor was storming at Sam again. "You *can't* go back to Texas yet! Do you want to kill yourself?"

"I have things to do."

Sam got as far as a little town near Nacogdoches. Once again someone grabbed him as he fell from his saddle. Soon another doctor was growling at him.

"You're going to stay in bed for at least a month! You'll stay if I have to tie you down."

The Texans elected Sam President. He got over 4000 votes. The next highest man got less than 800.

"You're in no condition to take on that job," the doctor said. "Wild men have been swarming into Texas. It'll take a man of iron to run this country. It'll be worse than fighting a war."

"I won't have to rule Texas very long," Sam told him. "The United States will take us into the Union."

But the United States said "No!" The North was fighting tooth and nail against admitting Texas. Another slave state? Never!

Chapter *11*

Two Monuments

Nine years later, in 1845, the United States admitted Texas. Sam felt as though he had just laid down a heavy load. He had been President of Texas twice. The doctor had been right. It had taken a man of iron to rule Texas.

Now he could have time to enjoy his family. He was married to a beautiful young woman from Alabama. He and Margaret had a little son.

"Now I'll have time to rest and enjoy little Sam," he said.

Margaret smiled. "You'll enjoy little Sam. I don't think you'll rest."

Sam was elected Senator from Texas. "I'll be lonely in Washington," he said.

"But you'll go," Margaret said to him. "Texas needs you."

The admission of Texas into the United States led to war with Mexico. When the war ended, America owned Texas, California, and all the land between them.

Sam knew there was danger of another war. The trouble between the North and South was getting worse. He was a Southerner, but he believed in the Union. For years, as Senator, Sam fought to hold the Union together.

In 1859 Texas elected him Governor. Day after day Sam made speeches in favor of the Union. Some people cheered. Others booed.

In February of 1861, Texas left the Union and joined the South. Sam walked the floor. "What can I do, Margaret? Will I turn against my country or turn against my state?"

"You'll do what you think is right," she said.

"If I don't promise to be true to the South, Texas will throw me out of the governor's chair."

"I've never seen you back down yet," Margaret said.

Sam let his beloved Texas throw him out of office. He went home to the little town of Huntsville.

"You'll have time for us now," the children said.

Sam grinned and hugged all of them he could hug at one time. He had eight children now. There were Sam, Jr., four little girls, then three more little boys. Andy was seven, Willie was three and Temple was a baby.

"Willie and I have fun," Andy said.

"I know," Sam said. "I had a brother named Willie."

In April the war began. "All at once," Sam thought, "I feel 100 years old."

The summer of 1863 he fell ill. "It's nothing," he said. "I'll get over it. I've got to! When the war's over, Texas will need me." But in July he died.

Today a monument marks the place where Sam saved Texas. The San Jacinto monument is the tallest one in the world. But the oldest monument to Sam Houston is a little log cabin near Maryville, Tennessee. It is the log schoolhouse where Sam "paid his own debt."